Alchemical Wisdom

Alchemical Wisdom

The Sayings of
Pir Vilayat Inayat Khan

Sulūk Press
New Lebanon, New York

Published by Sulūk Press,
an imprint of Omega Publications, Inc.
New Lebanon NY
www.omegapub.com

Cover photographs © Shutterstock.com
Cover design by Sandra Lillydahl
Photograph of Pir Vilayat Inayat Khan courtesy of
the Sufi Order International

This edition is printed on acid-free paper that meets
ANSI standard X39–48.

Vilayat Inayat Khan (1916–2004)
Alchemical Wisdom
The Sayings of Pir Vilayat Inayat Khan
Includes foreword, introduction, notes on author, index.
1.Inayat Khan, Vilayat.
2. Sufism II. Title

Library of Congress Control Number: 2015931065

Printed and bound in the United States of America
ISBN 978–1–941810–10–1

Contents

Foreword vii

Acknowledgments ix

Introduction *by Pir Vilayat Inayat Khan* ix

Alchemical Wisdom Sayings
  Distillation   3
  Essence   39
  Quintessence 73

About the Author 89

Index 93

Foreword

Pir Vilayat's retreat process was modeled on the ancient alchemical process of transmuting lead into gold, but here it is the human heart, which, purified of its dross, reflects the divine luminosity. Often a few words, a single idea, can prove the catalyst which moves this process from one stage to the next.

These sayings are classified according to three phases of the alchemical process:

Distillation
The pure expression of a quality

Essence
The heart of a quality

Quintessence
A quality in its universal significance

The uses of the Alchemical Wisdom sayings are as wide as one's imagination. Use them as daily meditations, as reflections of your soul's purpose, as guidance in a situation. For instance, sit quietly, trusting, holding one of your challenges in your heart. Be open...

Then choose a saying at random.

Put a favorite saying on your bathroom mirror, your car's dashboard, on your refrigerator. Add a quote as an inspiration in a letter to a friend. Choose a quote that is a mirror of your highest self. Share it. Then you could give it your own expression in a sound, a song, a movement or a drawing. Are you in a group that needs to make a decision? Sit quietly together and use the sayings to present a fresh perspective.

As Pir Vilayat reminds us,

Every moment is the chance of a lifetime.

Acknowledgments

Many thanks to Arifa Miller for recording and compiling the sayings; and to Professor Donald Graham for editing and arranging the original Alchemical Wisdom cards according to stages of alchemy, for providing this foreword, and for his permission to use his work for the present version. Thanks also to Lakshmi Nancy Barta-Norton for her assistance with production work. And most of all thanks to Pir Zia Inayat-Khan for his kind permission to publish his father's sayings.

Introduction

Following my father's [Hazrat Inayat Khan] message, I believe that to develop our being to its highest potential we need to discover our ideal and allow an inborn strength, a conviction in ourselves, to give us the courage toward developing this ideal. My deepest goal is to instill in those with whom I come into contact, a respect and tolerance for each world religion, recognizing the unity of ideals behind the diversity of forms. I believe in rising above distinctions and differences to appreciate the beauty and variety in people and cultures, and to uphold at all costs the dignity of every human being.

Pir Vilayat Inayat Khan

Alchemical Wisdom

Distillation

The pure expression of a quality

Unless we awaken them,
our capacities will always
lie dormant.

As long as you are convinced
of your opinion,
you will not rely upon
your intuition.

The mantra for
freedom from opinion is,
"What if?"

3

Base your being on a master,
but be creative.

See how your involvement
affects your freedom.

We foster ecstasy
by not being fooled by appearances
and rising to splendor.

The ultimate help to others
is to help them help themselves.

Guilt and resentment are two causes
for lack of joy.

"Turn the other cheek"
is absolutely irrational,
but makes the ultimate sense.

Do not pride yourself
on humility or poverty;
pride yourself
on your divine inheritance.

Meditation is for those
who don't love enough.

Let yourself reach into
the inner space
where you have contact
with all beings.

Spiritual practices
are planting seeds
in the subconscious,
which will eventually
bear fruit.

We are all handicapped
by our personal identity.

It's a discipline of mind
to see beauty in ugliness.

The power of detachment
is the power of silence,
of peace.

You can't be creative through will.
You must be in a state
where you need to create.

Don't be concerned about
being disloyal to your pain
by being joyous.

The mind is a wonderful instrument
of justification.

You can only help someone
if you know their problem yourself.
You have been through it,
and somehow you managed
to find freedom.

One needs something
to trigger off one's attunement
instead of one's thinking.

You have to get yourself into
a deep state of consciousness
to be able to rely on your intuition;
judgment is not reliable.

A little prayer on earth can ignite
an enormous cosmic celebration.

By accepting one's own shadow,
one gives unconditional love
to all beings.

If you seek for happiness
it will escape you.
Like a bird in the forest,
the more you chase it,
the further it will evade your grasp.

Consider every situation
which causes pain to your heart
as the way in which life
strikes this living receptacle
to make it vibrant, radiant,
alive, sensitive.

There's no such thing
as inanimate matter;
everything is a being.

The whole universe is
breathing as our breath;
we limit the process
by our assumption
that we are doing the breathing.

Overcome resentment
against people
and against God.

Music helps us bypass the mind.

Meditation is about learning
how to optimize
the potentialities of our being.

Anger is our defense system.

We can learn to put pain to good use.
This is the great art:
to capitalize on pain
to enhance inspiration.

The sense of sacredness
triggers off self-validation,
which in turn permits
personal creativity.

Spirituality is a tonic
for the injured psyche
rather than a sedative;
because the act of glorification
unveils the divine status
of one's own being.

At every move
our intentions are tested,
tested by life itself.

There is the despair of
not having what one wants,
and that is pain.
Pain is the first call of every heart.

You are sharing in
the totality of cosmic pain.
You are called upon to meet it in joy
instead of succumbing to self-pity.

See if you can get an answer
to your heart's greatest longing
by knocking upon the door
of your heart.

Think of God as an artist
who keeps changing His or Her mind.

What life is telling us is
to find freedom.

We can create four conditions to
be favorable to the revelation
of the Divine Intention
with silence, solitude,
fasting, and watchfulness.

All creativity starts with attunement,
and that attunement
finds its way into form.

Laughing at your own stupidity
is the first step toward sanity.

Some people bring out
the worst in us,
and perhaps that is good.

Physicists are now studying
the way glorification manifests
as the wish to reach
the throne of God.

You were born out of an act of glory,
and when you have found your being,
you can suddenly be transformed.

Cosmic programming
can't predict everything;
otherwise there is no progress.
The future is not entirely predictable.

Does one have the strength
to scan one's heart,
to provide excuses
for those who have
betrayed one's love?

Love transforms you
from death into life:
it quickens you to be able
to see where you cannot see
and feel where you cannot feel.

Meditation can very easily
become an ego trip;
and the only way to avoid this
is to preserve the dimension
of glorification in meditation.

A crystal is an expression of glory,
a prayer which has become
petrified emotion.

The greatest help in giving expression
to the depth which we never express
in our everyday life,
is to get into the consciousness
of a master, saint, a prophet.

One cannot "should" oneself,
or another person,
to be a hero.
But giving vent
to the latent hero in one
is a great fulfillment.

Resentment can degenerate
into hatred,
but it can be transmuted
by heroism.

Pain is as frost is to some plants:
it strengthens them.
Pain is very important
in the transformation of a person.

If we are indeed
the convergence of the universe
at all levels,
we are those spheres
which we think are out of our reach.

The human spirit lives on creativity
and dies in conformity and routine.

Instead of asking oneself,
"What do I need to do
to be successful?"
ask, "Am I being true to myself?"

Creativity is discovering
possibilities that have not yet
manifested in the universe,
by actuating them.

The same pain that
can blemish our personality,
can act as a creative force,
burnishing it into
an object of delight.

If human beings did not think
they depended upon God,
they would become monsters
(and they do).

The whole meaning of prayer
is that one has to ask
for something from God;
one can't imagine that
one can just do everything oneself.

An uncompromising person
is not balanced.

Unless one is prepared to restructure,
one is not part of
the evolutionary process.

When there is unconditional love,
one does not need
to find an alibi
for any person's behavior.

Think of all those whose hearts
you have quickened;
embrace them
with your being.

There is no point in
doing any meditation
until every little bit of grudge
against any being
has been completely uprooted.

The Tibetans say that the body
is a wonderful instrument
in which to promote illumination,
providing one knows how
to transform bodily functions.

Extend the walls of
your personal image
to include more
of the dimensions
of your divinity.

You can meet resentment
by finding room in your heart
for the one who has offended you.

The Sufis say,
"You have been invited to
the divine banquet,
and here you are,
crawling after crumbs."

Detachment keeps you
from being trapped.

The shadows of the world
rob the soul
of the vision of light.

By giving form through imagination –
vagabonding in realms of light –
we become both spectator
and participant.

There can be progress only
by shattering your understanding
to allow a greater understanding
to come through.

Our personality threads through
the consciousness of all beings,
and is the convergence of
the consciousness of all beings.

There are no limits to your being,
only those that you ascribe to yourself.

Our creativity is programming,
creating the software of the universe.

One source of power is
being very deeply moved
by the marvel of the universe.

Listen to
the secret language of nature.

If you neglect something,
it falls out of your control.

One is only ready to be a teacher
if one doesn't want to be a teacher.

Put your soul in charge of your life.

It is impossible to transmute
suffering into joy
without loving.

The only veil that separates
this world from the other world
is our mind.

Our thinking must be in harmony
with the thinking of the universe
to be valid.

In dealing with an ugly situation
beautifully, one is creating
circumstances to develop
the divinity of one's being.

We need to be uplifted by
an act of glorification.

It is impossible to radiate light
if one is harboring
resentment or guilt.

Every moment is
the chance of a lifetime.

We don't know what to do
with our freedom.

Instead of complaining,
see if there is not some sense
in what is happening.

That which seemed a problem
often avers itself to be the best thing
that could have happened to you.

Grace is the greatest gift:
no limitation,
a blank check.

To bring the sublime
into the mundane
is the greatest challenge there is.

The Sufis wish
for the body to participate
in the experience of the soul.

If you dedicate yourself to service,
the doors will open.

In our relationships
we need to uphold
that aspect of the person
which is the real person
and the soul
beyond their own self-doubt.

We are always trying to avoid a crisis,
so we procrastinate.
But the only way to avoid sclerosis
is to go ahead and have the crisis.

False humility is
an inverted form of pride.

Is someone hurting you?
Feel their suffering.

The more freedom there is
in a marriage,
the less need there is
for compromises.

You cannot always control your mind,
but you can give it direction.

Cast the light from your eyes
on a star.
In light-years of time,
the star receives your light.

Do not entertain guilt
that is not justified.

Be very truthful about resentment.
Are we ready to forgive?
We have to accept it
if we are not ready.

If we just simply react to
the challenge of life,
we are not using all
the resourcefulness
in our being.

In the beginning of creativity,
there is not just the personal emotion,
but the emotion of the universe.

A crisis can be good;
we unfold in a crisis,
and we are forced
to make a decision,
for better or worse.

For the sake of honesty
we have to avoid sanctimoniousness.
We can then convey
truth with integrity.

All creativity is a fluctuation
against static orderliness.

Everyone is in life
according to his realization.
And that is what meditation is about:
increasing realization.

Have the courage to manifest
who you are,
without taking refuge
in false humility.

Think in terms of resonance,
instead of concepts, facts,
pigeonholes.

Do not pay attention to clues
when you want to go
by your intuition.

One is only given
as much knowledge
as one can take.
That is the purpose of the veil.

One cannot help
a person who is suffering
unless one knows suffering
– and joy also.

Find accommodation
for all those hearts
that you have touched upon;
they have become
part of your being
forever.

We might be
the leading edge
in bringing about
the purpose of the universe.

Essence

The heart of a quality

There is a condition for
survival after death:
the truth body survives;
so if it's not very strong,
then there's not much survival.

I sometimes wonder
if our quest for awakening
is not the highest egotism.

Meditation takes us
to the dimension
where the irreconcilables
reconcile.

In the immaculate place of one's being
there is an innocent child
who can't be wounded, sullied
or tarnished.

Awakening, to the Sufis,
means the everywhere and always
manifests in the here and now.

The instant of time
is a sharp sword that frees you,
both from the conditioning of the past,
and the constraint that
you have imposed upon yourself
by your own planning.

Though you may not change it,
you can handle an ugly situation
beautifully.

What a risk God takes
in giving us freedom.

The ego is important
until one does not need it anymore.

We offer an obstacle to
God's experiencing fulfillment,
if we do not fully experience
our own identity.

How does one know
if one's intuition rings true?
By one's scruple about truthfulness,
one develops a sense
of authenticity.

If love for God seems
beyond your grasp,
then know that it is there
in every act of love.

If your heart is burning
in the ecstasy of love,
it will open the hearts
of all beings.

Perhaps the basic energy
of the universe is not light,
but ecstasy.
Light is ecstasy.

There are beings who
do not exist on the physical plane
but have their being on other planes.
We have our being on all planes.

There is a place in us
that can never be tarnished.

Perhaps the ultimate relaxation
is the relaxation
of our sense of identity.

The world of imagination
is the software of the universe.

Awakening and creativity are
the two poles of life's activity.

Sufis see the whole universe
as the divine nostalgia
for self-discovery.

Grace is very difficult to understand;
it's an expression of
freedom behind law.

If you think of God
as the Creator,
then you must also think of God
as the Sustainer,
because one is continually
being recreated.

The heart experiences emotion
at the sight of beauty,
whereas the soul experiences emotion
when it is faced with light.

To make God a reality,
we try to express in a form
that which is beyond form.

As one evolves,
one becomes
more and more spirit.

The clue is shifting
one's self-image, one's identity:
perceive yourself
as the essence.

Peace helps one overcome
the feeling of being subjected
to impressions from outside.

The human being is
the exemplification of God.

We are always concealing
our feelings
behind our thoughts.

The emotion of vastness frees one
from a sense of inadequacy.

We would not be creative
if our only purpose in life
is to be what we already are.

You are another me;
I am another you.

It is only when one is in a high state
that one's judgment is reliable.

When we want to change
another person,
we are showing a
lack of respect for them,
and what is important to them
in their past, present, and future.

Cherish others, uphold them;
guard them against humiliation.

Mastery consists in
never giving in to self-pity.

Let your peace
be materialized in actions.

Instead of lamenting your fate,
create your world.

Creativity is always taking a risk.

Of all the qualities in your being,
the one that is most God-like
is creativity.

We need a new way of communication
which is not experience
but communion.

We are the light of the stars.

Your power is limited
by your objective.
If your objective is service,
the power that comes through you
is unlimited.

The angels acquire wisdom
by incarnating.

Just imagine yourself as
the fulfillment of the Divine Purpose.

Discover God
instead of believing in God.

We must not confuse
our concept of God with God;
use it as a stepping-stone,
and then let it go.

When creativity is done with excellence,
splendor breaks through.

Ecstasy carries you to higher spheres
where you leave your will behind.

Every atom, planet, galaxy
is yearning for awakening;
not only you,
but the whole universe,
yearns to awaken.

Transformation is brought about
by being in the presence of God.

All creativity is the result
of imagination.

You become
what you concentrate on.
Concentrate on God
and you become God.

The power of your light
lies beyond the control of your will.

Divine Will and human will
are two dimensions
of the same thing.

Music is the language of the soul,
and therefore it communicates to us
something that could never
be communicated in words.

The symphony of the spheres
is made of all the cries of glee
upon discovery.

The ultimate mantram is
the sound of the cry of glory.

Have your strength
in your heart,
not in your head.

Pain makes the soul sincere.

Shake your soul!
Awaken it from slumber!
The time has come to awaken
to your divine being.

The divine in us
is what we can rely on.

In some challenging situations
you can be very kind and gentle
by not giving in.

You can't know the defects of a person
without having them yourself.

Can you imagine a being
whose light is more radiant than suns?
That's an archangel.
You carry the inheritance of that being.

The ultimate meditation is
"Who am I?"

The thought of dissolving,
not holding on,
overcomes greed.

Service is the opposite of greed.

The problem is not the situation,
but how one handles the situation.

You have to find
enough freedom
in yourself
to be able to free others.

The whole of life is a process
whereby the unmanifest
becomes manifest.

When one loves,
one abstains from judging.
The "knowledge" that
you have of a person,
without love for that person,
is judgment.

A closed heart means
not trusting oneself to love.

When the sun is not in the sky,
then one can see the stars.

The magnificence of the Universe
is in you.

Science deals with
predictables;
creativity deals with
unpredictables.

The only way to hear
the voice of glory
is to sing it ourselves.

Freedom gives infinite power;
it can move mountains.

Healing is a combination
of joy and peace.
Joy in our relationship
with the outside;
and peace in our discovery
of the springhead of our being.

Your domain is as wide
as the influence of your soul.
The higher the soul is attuned,
the greater the domain.

Our soul can be robbed
of its power
by resentment.

Your intuition is the revelation
of your own spirit.

The purpose of imagination
is to transform the uncreated
into a form.

The light of awareness,
the light of consciousness,
arises out of a broken heart.
The heart, by breaking,
becomes an ocean,
accommodating all beings.

Light arises in your soul
as a consequence of
the striking of the heart.

The universe is breathing in you,
on several planes,
at the same time.

Christ dances on the cross.
He doesn't hang there–
times have changed.

Your circumstances are a reflection
of what you are in yourself.

Spiritual progress comes
by changing one's point of view.

We are the transducer between
the universal light
and universal matter.

Hear the sound of the universe
in your heart.

There is no door
that the heart cannot open,
when it has become so living
that it is the Divine Ocean.

The first principle in healing is joy.

We don't love the tree
because of its beauty,
but for the being of the tree.

Get into a state of passive volition,
which means unintentionally
pursuing one's intention.

Find your relationship
with the universe,
which has nothing to do
with space at all.

Let yourself grasp immensity,
the immensity of which
you are an expression.

The rishi can observe a flower
opening under his glance.
That can be your experience.

We are the convergence
of the whole universe.
We all have a great need
for immensity.

Perhaps it is written
in our programming:
to transmute personal love
into divine emotion.

The atoms themselves are endowed
with intelligence, consciousness,
and even emotion.

If you cannot love all beings,
you can express divine love
in forgiveness,
which means to purify your heart
of grudges against any being.

Truth will make you free,
but it will also make you suffer.

Music teaches us that conflicts
are part of harmony.

One can get into the emotion
that has become a flower;
that is the experience of the mystic
and the dervish.

Even our bodies are endowed
with the rhythms of
the symphony of the spheres,
the language of God.

We can discover in ourselves
what we perceive in the cosmos.

We can reach any being,
any person,
from inside ourselves.

Truthfulness develops
intuition.

Have the courage to face
the light of your own being.

It is wise to balance mastery
with intuition.

The best use of intuition
is as a warning.

One cannot reach one's highest self
without having found peace in oneself.

The beauty that comes through
the mind inspired by ecstasy
is monumental.

Creativity is the thrust of ecstasy
and making it an actuality
in our lives.

Ecstasy is triggered off
every time one rises above oneself.

We can realize ourselves
as extensions of the universe
as God.

God's presence is all-pervading,
whether there is manifestation or not;
it is very mysterious.

Think of yourself as a soul
instead of as a person.

The purpose of life is that
God should attain through you
a further advance in
the evolution of the universe.

Quintessence

A quality in its universal significance

Let your power come through
as the manifestation of truth.

Experience yourself
as the Divine Intention.

Experience the condition
of the universe inside yourself.

The only evil is harming
another or yourself,
another soul
or your own soul.

Always be conscious of
your eternal being.

Divine Creativity is completed
by human creativity.

We are a dome in which
the music of the spheres resounds.

The whole purpose of life is
for God to emerge as us.

We discover beauty
as we create it.

Ecstasy is total involvement,
taking the plunge,
relentlessly coping with the odds,
dauntlessly riding
the tide of adversity.

Communicate beauty by
being in love with beauty,
which means being in love with God.
That is the ultimate Reality.

There's no outside,
there is no inside;
once the heart has become
the ocean of life,
it accommodates
all things and all beings.

The whole universe was created
for the purpose of illumination.

Life attains its summit
in magnanimity.

To be a lover
one needs to be a master.

Think of peace as power.

There are no objects,
only beings!

To gain insight, the mystic goes
to the depths of the universe.

We are not here for ourselves.

You are the artist,
you are the raw material,
you are the work of art,
and you are the reality
behind the work of art.

Never think of yourself
as an individual different
from God.

Face God and allow
the divine action of God
to happen in you.

The more conscious we are
of radiating light,
the more light we radiate.

It is our ecstasy
in the act of glorification
that gives us access
to the level of pure splendor.

The archangel of your being
is your own soul.

Love is the wine
of the Divine Intoxication.

Your heart is no longer just your heart,
since it has become the heart
of the Divine Beloved.

See your problems in the light
of what is happening
in the whole universe.

Divine love is the effulgence
behind all creation,
behind all phenomena,
and the light in the heart
of those you love,
whose light you enhance
by your love.

Your own heart is the key
to the hearts of all.

The universe is breathing
as you.

When you are in a state of ecstasy
your thoughts are creative;
then one's emotions and movements
reveal a cosmic harmony.

We not only transmit
the thinking of the universe;
we contribute to that thinking
in a personal way.

God is continually
performing new acts of freedom,
freeing people from the rigidity of Law.
That is grace.

Grace means the opposite of Law.

God seeks fulfillment
in the human being.

The emotion of glorification
comes when we let
the divine action take over.
We prepare by purification,
by lending ourselves
to the divine operation.

The discovery of
the more transcendental dimensions
of one's being is gained by doing:
dedicating oneself to service
and acting on it.

Be kind to your soul;
your soul's need
is exaltation.

Not just the eyes, but the heart itself,
casts light upon all things.

That which clarifies the soul
is truthfulness.

We betray ourselves
when we yearn to find
a Beloved outside.

God cannot be good and perfect
at the same time.

You experience yourself
as matter experiencing spirit;
and you experience yourself
as spirit experiencing matter.

One experiences ecstasy
when one discovers
the Creator in one,
as oneself.

Ecstasy is the magic
out of which life is born;
the word that opens doors
into unpredictable perspectives.

We are the image of God,
and God is our image.

We get caught up in
the light that is seen;
we are also
the light that sees.

The key to the plane of splendor
is not understanding,
but ecstasy.

God finds completion
in the human being.

The whole past of the universe
is present in your being.

When we enter into
the mind of God,
we can act in a way
that enhances
the Divine Intention.

Ultimately, the only thing
that makes sense in life
is glorification.

We come to identify with
our planetary, solar, galactic,
and even angelic, inheritance
as the boundaries of consciousness
dissolve.

Out of love for your potentialities,
God descended
from the solitude
of unknowing.

Everything is linked
with everything else,
inextricably.

There's no threshold
between us
and the universe.

Rebirth takes place
in the act of surrender.

God discovers His perfection
in human imperfection.

God cannot be limited
by manifestation.

Pir Vilayat Inayat Khan

Pir Vilayat Inayat Khan (1916–2004) was the eldest son and spiritual successor of Hazrat Pir-O-Murshid Inayat Khan, the first Sufi master to teach in the West. Vilayat Inayat Khan was born in England and raised in France. He was educated at the Sorbonne, Oxford, and École Normale de Musique de Paris. During World War II he served in the British Royal Navy and was assigned the duties of mine sweeping during the invasion at Normandy. His sister, Noor Inayat Khan served in the French section of Britain's SOE (Special Operations Executive) as a radio operator. She was captured and executed in 1944 at Dachau concentration camp.

After the war, Pir Vilayat pursued his spiritual training by studying with masters of many different religious traditions throughout India and the Middle East. While honoring the initiatic tradition of his predecessors, in his teachings Pir Vilayat continually adapted traditional Eastern spiritual practices in keeping with the evolution of Western consciousness. Throughout his life, he was an avid student of many religious and spiritual traditions and incorporated the rich mystical heritage of East and West into his teachings, adding to it the scholarship of the West in music, science, and psychology. He taught in the tradition of Universal Sufism, which views all religions as rays of light from the same sun.

Pir Vilayat initiated and participated in numerous international and interfaith conferences promoting understanding and world peace as well as convening spiritual and scientific leaders for public dialogues. In 1975 he founded the Abode of the Message, a central residential community of the Sufi Order International, a conference and retreat center, and a center of esoteric study. He also founded Omega Institute for Holistic Studies, a flourishing learning center, and published many books on aspects of meditation and realization.

For more information on
Pir Vilayat Inayat Khan
and the Sufi Order International,
please see
www.sufiorder.org

Index

A

actuality 68
adversity 75. *See also* challenge
alchemy vii. *See also* transformation, transmutation.
angels 50, 86; archangel 55, 78
anger 11
appearances 4
art 11, 77; artist 13, 77. *See also* beauty, creativity.
assumption 10
atoms 51, 64
attunement 8, 14, 59
authenticity 42. *See also* truth.
awakening 3, 39–40, 44, 51, 54. *See also* illumination, realization, revelation.
awareness 60. *See also* consciousness.

B

balance 20, 67. *See also* harmony.
beauty ix, 6, 26, 41, 45, 63, 67, 74–75. *See also* art, perfection, harmony
behavior 21
belief 50. *See also* concepts, religion.
Beloved 79, 83
betrayal 15, 83. *See also* disloyalty.
bird 9
body 22, 29, 66; truth body 39. *See also* incarnation.
breath 10; breathing 10, 61, 80

C

capacities 3. *See also* possibilities, potentialities.
catalyst vii. *See also* transformation, transmutation.
celebration *See* cosmic celebration.
challenges viii, 28, 32, 55. *See also* crisis, problem.
chance viii, 27
change 13, 41, 48, 61

child 40

Christ 61

circumstances 26, 61

clue 34, 46

communication 49, 53, 75

communion 49

completion 74, 85. *See also* fulfillment, perfection.

compromises 30; uncompromising 20

concentration 52. *See also* meditation.

concepts 34. 51. *See also* belief, thoughts.

conditioning 13, 39–40, 73

conflicts 65

conformity 18

consciousness 8, 17, 24, 60, 64, 74, 78, 86, 89. *See also* awareness, psyche, revelation, state, transcendental dimensions.

constraint 40. *See also* limitation.

control 25, 31, 52; control of your will 52. *See also* discipline, mastery.

convergence 18, 24, 64

cosmos 66; cosmic celebration 8; cosmic harmony 80; cosmic pain 12; cosmic programming 15. *See also* universe, world.

courage ix, 33, 67. *See also* hero, power, strength.

creativity 4, 7, 11, 13–14, 18–19, 24, 26, 32–33, 44–45, 47, 49, 51–52, 58, 68, 74, 76, 79–80. *See also* art, imagination, inspiration, possibilities, potentialities.

Creator, the 45, 83

crisis 30, 32. *See also* challenge; problem.

cross 61

crystal 16

D

death 16, 39

decision viii, 32

dedication 29, 82

defects, personal 55

defense 11

delight 19. *See also* happiness, joy.

dervish 65. *See also* Sufis.

despair 12. *See also* pain, suffering.

detachment 6, 23

development ix, 26, 42, 66

dignity ix. *See also* respect.

discipline 6. *See also* control,

mastery.

discovery ix, 19, 44, 50, 53, 59, 66, 74, 82–83, 87. *See also* realization, revelation.

disloyalty 7. *See also* betrayal.

dissolving 56, 86

diversity ix

divinity 11, 22, 26, 54; divine action 78, 81; divine banquet 23; divine being 54; Divine Creativity 74; divine emotion, 64; divine inheritance, 5; Divine Intention 13, 73, 85; Divine Intoxication 79; Divine Love 65, 79; divine luminosity vii, divine nostalgia 44; Divine Ocean 62; divine operation 81; Divine Purpose 50; Divine Will 53. *See also* God.

domain 59

dome 74

doors 13, 29, 62, 84

E

earth 8. *See also* world.

ecstasy 4, 42–43, 51, 67–68, 75, 78, 80, 83–84. *See also* delight, exaltation, joy.

effulgence 79. *See also* glory, light, luminosity, radiance, splendor.

ego 16, 41; egotism 39. *See also* identity, personality, self.

emotion 16, 32, 45, 47, 64–65, 80–81; emotion of the universe 32. *See also* feelings.

essence vii, 46

eternal being 74. *See also* soul.

evil 73

evolution 20, 46, 89; evolution of the universe 69. *See also* progress, transformation, transmutation.

exaltation 82. *See also* ecstasy, glory.

eyes 31, 82. *See also* glance, vision.

F

facts 34

fasting 13

feelings 46–47. *See also* emotion.

flower 64–65

forest 9

forgiveness 31, 65. *See also* judg-
    ment, reconciliation.
form ix, 14, 23, 45, 60. *See
    also* body, incarnation,
    manifestation.
freedom 3–4, 7, 13, 27, 30,
    40–41, 44, 47, 56, 58,
    81, 85
fruit 6
fulfillment 17, 41, 50, 81. *See
    also* completion, long-
    ing, purpose, success.
future 15, 48

G

gentle 55
glance 64. *See also* eyes,
    vision.
glee 53. *See also* happiness,
    joy.
glorification 11, 14, 16, 27,
    78, 81, 85. *See also* ec-
    stasy, exaltation, glory.
glory 15–16, 53, 58. *See also*
    effulgence, glori-
    fication, radiance,
    splendor.
God 10, 13, 20, 41–42, 45,
    49–52, 68–69, 74–75,
    77–78, 81, 83–87;
    concept of God 51;
    exemplification of God
    46; God's presence 52,

68; image of God 84;
    language of God 66;
    mind of God 13, 85;
    throne of God 14. *See
    also* divinity.
gold vii
goodness 14, 83
grace 28, 44, 81
greed 56
grudge 21, 65. *See also* re-
    sentment.
guidance vii
guilt 4, 27, 31

H

happiness 9. *See also* delight,
    glee, joy, laughing..
harm 73. *See also* evil, pain,
    suffering.
harmony 26, 65, 80. *See also*
    balance, music.
hatred 17
head 54. *See also* mind,
    thoughts.
healing 59, 62
heart vii–viii, 9, 12–13, 15,
    21–22, 35, 37, 42, 45,
    54, 57, 60, 62, 65, 75,
    79–80, 82; broken
    heart 60; door of your
    heart 13. *See also*
    longing, love.
help 4, 7, 17, 34, 46. *See also*

service.
hero 17; heroism 17. *See also* courage.
honesty 33
human being ix, 46, 81, 85; human creativity 74; human imperfection 87; human spirit 18; human will 53
humiliation 48
humility 5; false humility 30, 33

I

identity 6, 41, 43, 46, 86. *See also* ego, personality, self.
illumination 22, 76. *See also* awakening, light, luminosity, radiance.
image 22, 46, 84; of God 84
imagination vii, 23, 44, 50, 52, 55, 60. *See also* creativity, possibilities, potentialities.
immensity 63–64
imperfection 87
impressions 46
inadequacy 47
incarnation 50. *See also* body, form, manifestation.
inheritance 5, 55, 86
inner space 5

innocence 40
insight 77. *See also* intuition, knowledge.
inspiration viii, 11, 67
instant of time 40. *See also* moment, time.
integrity 33
intelligence 64. *See also* knowledge, mind, thoughts, wisdom.
intention 12, 63; Divine Intention 13, 73, 85
intuition 3, 8, 34, 42, 60, 66–67. *See also* insight, knowledge, vision.
involvement 4, 75
irreconcilables 39

J

joy 4, 7, 12, 26, 34, 59, 62. *See also* delight, ecstasy, glee, happiness.
judgment 8, 48, 57. *See also* forgiveness, lack of respect, reconciliation.
justification 7, 31

K

kindness 55, 82
knowledge 34, 57. *See also* intelligence, understanding, wisdom.

L

lack of respect 48. *See also* judgment.

language of nature, 25; language of God 66; language of the soul 53

laughing 14

law 44, 81

life 9, 12–13, 16–17, 25, 32–33, 44, 57, 75–76, 84–85, 89; lifetime viii, 27; purpose of life 47, 69, 74.. *See also* quickening.

light 23, 27, 31, 43, 45, 50, 52, 55, 60, 62, 67, 78–79, 82, 84, 90; light that is seen 84; light that sees 84. *See also* effulgence, illumination, luminosity, radiance.

limitation 10, 24, 28, 50, 87. *See also* constraint.

longing 13. *See also* fulfillment, wish.

love 5, 15–16, 26, 42, 57, 63–65, 75, 79, 86; Divine Love 65, 79; love for God 42; lover 76; unconditional love 8, 21. *See also* Beloved, heart, longing.

luminosity vii. *See also* effulgence illumination, light, radiance.

M

magic 84

magnanimity 76

magnificence 58

manifestation 14, 19, 33, 40, 57, 68, 73, 87. *See also* body, form, incarnation.

mantra(m) 3, 53

marriage 30. *See also* relationship.

marvel 25

master 4, 17, 76, 89. *See also* mastery.

mastery 48, 67. *See also* control, discipline, master.

meditation vii, 5, 10, 16, 21, 33, 39, 55, 90. *See also* concentration, mantra, practices, spirituality.

mind 6–7, 10, 26, 31, 67; mind of God 12, 85. *See also* consciousness, intelligence, knowledge, sanity, thoughts, wisdom.

moment viii, 27. *See also*

instant of time.

music 10, 53, 65, 90; music of the spheres 74. *See also* harmony, resonance, sound, symphony of the spheres.

mystic 65, 77; mystical heritage 90. *See also* dervish, meditation, Sufis.

N

nature 25

O

objective 50. *See also* longing, purpose.

ocean 60, 75. Divine Ocean 62.

offense 22

opinion 3. *See also* perspective, point of view.

orderliness 33. *See also* law, routine.

P

pain 7, 9, 11–12, 18–19, 54. *See also* despair, harm, suffering.

passive volition 63

past 40, 48, 85

peace 6, 46, 49, 59, 67, 76, 90

perfection 83, 87. *See also* art, beauty, completion, fulfillment.

personality 19, 24, 80; personal image 22. *See also* ego, identity, psyche, self, subconscious.

perspective viii, 84. *See also* opinion, point of view.

physicists 14

planes (of existence) 43, 61, 84. *See also* incarnation, manifestation.

planning 40

plants 18; planting seeds 6. *See also* flower, forest, fruit, tree.

point of view 61. *See also* opinion, perspective.

possibilities 19. *See also* capacities, creativity, potentialities.

potentialities ix, 10, 86. *See also* capacities, creativity, possibilities.

poverty 5

power 6, 25, 50, 52, 58–59, 73, 76. *See also* courage, strength.

practices, spiritual 6, 89. *See also* meditation.

prayer 8, 16, 20

prediction 15, 58
present (time) 48
pride 5, 30. *See also* sancti-
    moniousness.
problem 7, 28, 56, 79. *See
    also* crisis, challenge.
procrastination 30
programming 15, 24, 64. *See
    also* software of the
    universe.
progress 15, 24, 61. *See also*
    evolution, transforma-
    tion.
prophet 17
psyche 11
purity vii, 1, 78; purification
    vii, 65, 81
purpose vii, 34, 47, 60, 69,
    74, 76; Divine Purpose
    50; purpose of the
    universe 35. *See also*
    fulfillment, objective.

Q

qualities vii, 1, 49
quickening 16, 21. *See also*
    life, spirit, vibrancy.

R

radiance 9, 27, 55, 78. *See
    also* effulgence, glory,
    illumination, light,
luminosity, splendor.
reaction 32
reality 45, 75, 77
realization 33, 68, 90. *See also*
    awareness, awaken-
    ing, consciousness,
    discovery.
rebirth 87. *See also* transfor-
    mation.
reconciliation 39. *See also*
    forgiveness.
reflection vii, 61
relationship 29, 59, 63.
    See also forgivenes,
    judgment, marriage,
    reconciliation.
relaxation 43
religion ix, 90. *See also* belief.
relying (on) 3, 8, 54
resentment 4, 10, 22, 27, 31,
    59. *See also* forgive-
    ness, grudge, reconcil-
    iation.
resonance 34. *See also* sound.
resourcefulness 32
respect ix, 48. *See also* dig-
    nity.
restructure 20
revelation 13, 60, 80. *See also*
    awakening, conscious-
    ness, discovery, vision,
    wisdom.
rhythms 66

rishi 64
routine 18. *See also* orderliness.

S

sacredness 11
saint 17
sanctimoniousness 33. *See also* pride.
sanity 14
science 58, 90. *See also* physicists.
sclerosis 30
seeds 6
self, highest viii, 67
self-discovery 44;
self-doubt 29
self-image 46
self-pity 12, 48
self-validation 11.
sense 5, 28, 85
sensitivity 9
service 29, 50, 56, 82. *See also* help.
shadow 8; shadows of the world 23
shattering 24
silence 6, 13
sincerity 54
software of the universe 24, 44. *See also* programming.

solitude 13; of unknowing 86
soul vii, 23, 25, 29, 45, 53–54, 59–60, 69, 73, 78, 82. *See also* eternal being.
sound 53; sound of the universe 62. *See also* music, resonance, rhythm.
spectator 23
spheres 18, 51, 53, 66, 74. *See also* transcendental dimension, universe.
spirit 18, 46, 60, 83. *See also* spirituality, quickening.
spirituality ii, 6, 11, 61, 89–90; spiritual practices 6, 89; spiritual progress 61. *See also* meditation, revelation, mystic, soul, spirit, Sufis, vision.
splendor 4, 51, 78, 84. *See also* effulgence, glory, luminosity, radiance.
springhead of our being 59
stars 31, 50, 57
state 7–8, 48, 63, 80
strength ix, 15, 18, 54. *See also* courage, power.
stupidity 14
subconscious 6. *See also* self, personality.

sublimity 20

success 19. *See also* fulfillment, purpose.

suffering 26, 30, 34, 65. *See also* despair, pain.

Sufis 23, 29, 40, 44, 89–90. *See also* dervish, mystic.

sun 55, 57, 90

surrender 87

survival (after death) 39

Sustainer, the 45

sword 40

symphony of the spheres 53, 66. *See also under music*, music of the spheres.

T

teacher 25

thoughts 47, 56, 80; thinking 8, 26; thinking of the universe 26, 80. *See also* concepts, head, knowledge, mind.

threshold 87

Tibetans 22

time 31, 40, 54, 61, 68, 83. *See also* future, moment, past, present.

tolerance ix

transcendental dimensions 82. *See also* consciousness, spheres.

transducer 62

transformation 15–16, 18, 22, 52, 60. *See also* alchemy, evolution, rebirth, transmutation.

transmutation vii, 17, 26, 64. *See also* alchemy, evolution, transformation.

tree 63

truth 19, 33, 73; truth body 39; truthfulness 31, 42, 82. *See also* authenticity.

turn the other cheek 5

U

ugliness 6, 26, 41

uncreated 60. *See also* unmanifest.

understanding 24, 44, 84, 90. *See also* awareness, forgiveness, knowledge, wisdom.

unity of ideals ix

universality vii, 62, 91

universe 10, 18–19, 24–26, 32, 35, 43–44, 51, 58, 61–64, 68–69, 73, 76–77, 79–80, 85, 87. *See also* cosmos, spheres, world.

unmanifest 57. *See also* uncreated.
unpredictable (the) 58, 84

V

vastness 47
veil 26, 34; unveiling 11
vibrancy 9. *See also* life,
   quickening.
vision 23. *See also* eyes, revelation.

W

warning 67
watchfulness 13
will 7, 51–53
wine 79
wisdom 50. *See also* awareness, knowledge, reve-
   lation, understanding.
wish 14, 29. *See also* fulfillment, longing.
words 53, 84
world ix, 23, 26, 44, 49, 91.
   See also cosmos, earth,
   universe.